EXPERTS IN ENGINEERING

WAYLAND
www.waylandbooks.co.uk

First published in Great Britain
in 2018 by Wayland
Copyright © Hodder & Stoughton, 2018

Wayland
An imprint of Hachette
Children's Group
Part of Hodder & Stoughton
Carmelite House
50 Victoria Embankment
London EC4Y 0DZ

Series editor: Elise Short
Produced by Tall Tree Ltd
Written by: Rob Colson
Designer: Ben Ruocco

ISBN: 978 1 5263 08399
10 9 8 7 6 5 4 3 2 1

An Hachette UK Company
www.hachette.co.uk
www.hachettechildrens.co.uk

Printed and bound in China

MIX
Paper from
responsible sources
FSC
www.fsc.org   FSC® C104740

Picture credits
t–top, b–bottom, l–left, r–right, c–centre,
front cover–fc, back cover–bc
All images courtesy of Dreamstime.com and all
icons made by Freepik from www.flaticon.com,
unless indicated:

Inside front Aleksey Legkostupov; fc, bc Deviney;
fcr Stedata; fcl, 14b Leungphotography; bccl,
14br Brooklyn Museum Collection; 3t Igor
Netkov; 4b ShareAlike 3.0 Unported (CC BY-SA
3.0); 4-5 Jgroup; 6br Evolution1088; 6b
Thomaseder; 6-7 Witr; 8-9 Shutterstock.com/cyo
bo; 9tr Georgios; 10bl Johnsroad7; 10-11 Dmitryp;
11c Dennis G. Jarvis; 12-13 Shutterstock.com/
iwonag; 13t Dmytro Adazhiy; 16-17 Rhodesfilm;
18-19 Adfoto; 19tl Arkela; 19tr Shutterstock.com/
Zern Liew; 19b Sonulkaster; 20-21 Kmiragaya;
21tl Mxk; 21c ShareAlike 3.0 Unported (CC BY-SA
3.0); 22b Aneese; 24-25 Pn_photo; 25tr Halberg;
26b NASA; 27t Galina Balashova Archives;
27bl NASA; 28b Olena Ostapenko; 28-29 U.S.
Navy photo/Ensign Dusan Ilic; 29t ShareAlike
4.0 International (CC BY-SA 4.0)

Every effort has been made to acknowledge every
image source but the publisher apologises for any
unintentional errors or omissions that will be
corrected in future editions of this book.

CONTENTS

THE ENGINEERING CHALLENGE

Civil engineers design and build structures such as bridges, buildings and tunnels. Architects and engineers need to ensure the structures they design and build are strong enough to withstand challenges such as high winds or earthquakes.

The test of time

The Arkadiko Bridge in Greece was built more than 3,000 years ago for use by horse-drawn chariots. It formed part of a road linking the cities of Tiryns and Epidauros. The stone structure has survived the test of time, and the bridge is still used today.

Simple machines

With no engines or electricity to help them, builders in the ancient world used simple machines such as ramps and pulleys to help them lift heavy stone or wood into position. Huge teams of men were needed to do the work. Today, giant cranes with powerful motors do the heavy lifting work.

Green engineering

Concerned about polluting the planet, architects are engineering buildings that are kind to the environment. In Singapore, giant 50-m-high vertical gardens called 'supertrees' have been built in a park in the centre of the city. The supertrees generate electricity and collect rainwater. They are also home to a huge collection of rare plants.

A crane lifts a huge metal girder into place as the frame of a high-rise building is constructed.

Read on to discover the challenges that engineers have overcome through the ages. The answers to questions in the projects are found on page 31.

GREAT PYRAMID OF GIZA

The Great Pyramid was built in 2560 BCE. The tallest of three pyramids in Giza, Egypt, at 146 m, it was the highest building in the world for the next 3,800 years. It is the oldest of the structures known as the Seven Wonders of the World, and the only one still standing.

A square pyramid

The pyramid has a square base and four triangular sides that meet at a single point at the top. This shape is called a square pyramid. Before constructing the pyramid, Egyptian engineers had to level the ground to within a fraction of a centimetre's accuracy to create a firm foundation. They then began constructing the pyramid out of pre-cut blocks of stone.

Building blocks

The Great Pyramid is made from 2.3 million separate blocks of stone, which each weigh up to 15 tonnes – the weight of four large elephants. Some of this stone was cut from quarries 900 km away, and transported to the building site along the River Nile. The blocks were precisely carved – using copper chisels – to fit together along joints just 0.5 mm wide.

How was it built?

Historians still debate over how the Great Pyramid was built. It is likely that tens of thousands of workers were involved, and that it took many years to complete. The stones were dragged into position along ramps, but we do not know how they were raised up the ramps, as the Egyptians did not use wheels or pulleys.

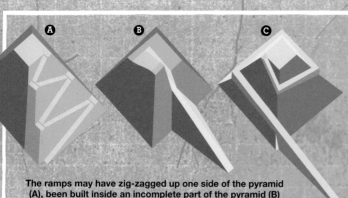

The ramps may have zig-zagged up one side of the pyramid (A), been built inside an incomplete part of the pyramid (B) or spiralled on top of the structure (C).

Burial chambers

The pyramids were built as tombs for the pharaohs (kings). The Great Pyramid is Pharaoh Khufu's tomb. Inside the Great Pyramid, three chambers have been found: a large chamber known as the King's Chamber, a smaller one known as the Queen's Chamber and an unfinished Lower Chamber. In 2017, scientists discovered a hidden passage in the pyramid. It remains a mystery what this passage was used for.

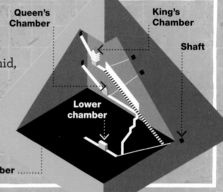

Queen's Chamber

King's Chamber

Shaft

Lower chamber

Subterranean chamber

The Great Pyramid is flanked by smaller ones.

PROJECT: RAMP IT UP

The steeper a ramp is, the more force you need to drag an object up it. Let's investigate this further.

You will need: a flat piece of wood, some books, a cup, a piece of string, an apple, some coins

1. Make a ramp by resting the wood on a pile of books.
2. Attach the cup to the string and wrap it around the apple.
3. Hang the cup over the back of the ramp and start loading it with pennies. How many coins does it take to move the apple?

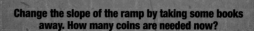

Change the slope of the ramp by taking some books away. How many coins are needed now?

LAYING DOWN TRACKS

Steam-powered locomotives were invented in the early 19th century, marking the start of the railway age. These heavy machines needed parallel iron tracks to run on. The first tracks to carry passenger trains were built in England in the early 19th century.

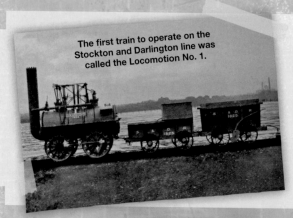

The first train to operate on the Stockton and Darlington line was called the Locomotion No. 1.

The first line

The first public railway, the Stockton and Darlington Railway, opened in 1825. It was 40 km long, and trains took two hours to complete the journey between the two towns. Railways proved very popular, and just 20 years later, more than 3,000 km of track had been laid across Great Britain.

George Stephenson (1781–1848)

Stephenson (pictured right) was an English engineer who built some of the first steam locomotives and railway lines for them to travel along. For the Stockton and Darlington Railway, Stephenson set the gauge of his track (the distance between the parallel rails) to 1.4 m (4 ft 8). After the success of Stephenson's early lines, other railways adopted his gauge, and most railways around the world still use it today.

<-·········· Gauge ··········>

Expansion joint

When objects heat up, they expand. Railway engineers must allow for this, and leave a gap of a few millimetres between sections of rail to allow for expansion during hot weather. The clickety-clack sound of a train is made when the wheels pass over expansion joints.

Expansion joint

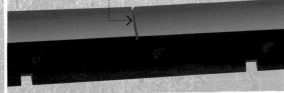

Magnetic tracks

The first trains were powered by steam engines. These were later replaced by diesel engines and electric engines. Today, maglev trains are powered by the tracks they run along. The trains hover above a magnetic track, known as a guideway. A changing magnetic field in the guideway pushes the trains along at up to 600 km/h, making them the fastest trains ever.

PROJECT:
HEATED NEEDLE

Explore expansion in action in this experiment to be done with an adult as it involves a naked flame.

You will need: a knitting needle, a cork, two bottles, a sewing needle, a candle, a straw, a pile of books

1. Set up the apparatus as in the diagram, with the knitting needle pushed into the cork in one bottle, and balancing on a second bottle.
2. Stick the sewing needle through the straw and rest the sewing needle underneath the knitting needle to form a cross, resting on the top of the second bottle.
3. Now heat the knitting needle with the candle.

Sewing needle forming a cross with knitting needle

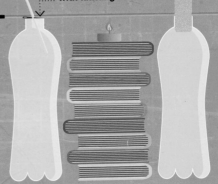

What happens to the straw as the needle is heated?

WARNING LIGHTS

Lighthouses are towers that emit a beam of light to warn of hazardous waters or rocks. The earliest lighthouses were open fires of burning wood or coal mounted on platforms. The fires were replaced by oil lamps in the 18th century, and electric bulbs were brought in from 1875.

Augustin-Jean Fresnel (1788–1827)

This French physicist invented a lens that multiplied the luminosity (brightness) of lighthouses by four times. First used in the Cordouan Lighthouse, France, in 1823, the Fresnel lens produced a concentrated beam of light that could be seen from 30 km away.

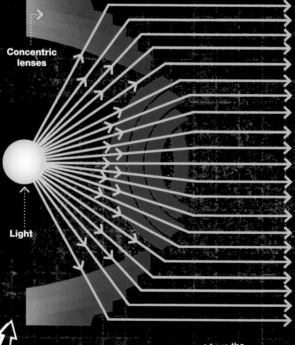

Concentric lenses

Light

The lens refracts (bends) the light coming out from the bulb into a powerful beam of parallel light rays. It is made of concentric rings. Each ring refracts the light a little more than the ring inside it.

Keeping away

Lighthouse warning lights rotate to send a beam in all directions. This makes the light appear to be flashing when seen from a ship. Different lighthouses rotate at different speeds, meaning that the captain of a ship can tell which lighthouse they are near by the frequency of the flashes. The light bulb used in each lighthouse has a set brightness, so captains can judge their distance by the brightness of the flash.

 Like most lighthouses, Cape Egmont Lighthouse in New Zealand is now fully automated. Up to 1986, a lighthouse keeper lived there to maintain the light.

Range lights

Lighthouses can be paired up to help ships navigate the right course into a dangerous harbour. Called range lights, or leading lights, they are positioned in such a way that they line up one above the other when the ship is on the correct course.

PROJECT:
HOW BRIGHT IS THE LIGHT?

Measure how the brightness of a light reduces rapidly as you move away from it.

You will need: a torch, some books, paper, a tape measure, tape, calculator

1. Focus the beam of the torch as tightly as you can. Place it forizontally on a stack of books on a table.
2. Mark distances with the tape from the torch at 5-cm intervals, from 5 cm to 25 cm.
3. Tape a piece of white paper to the side of another book, and hold the paper to the light at each distance. Trace a circle around each beam.
4. Measure the diameter of each circle and use a calculator to do the following calculation: square the diameter (multiply it by itself), then multiply it by 0.785. This gives the area of the circle.

What happens to the areas of the circles as you move further away from the light? If you double the distance, how many times bigger is the area of the circle?

BORING A TUNNEL

The Thames Tunnel under the River Thames in London, was the first tunnel to be built under a navigable river – a river large enough for ships to use. The tunnel took 18 years to complete, and opened to the public in 1843.

Sir Marc Isambard Brunel (1769–1849)

The French-born engineer in charge of digging the Thames Tunnel, Brunel, invented a special tunnelling shield for the job. The iron shield protected workers at the tunnel-face. Once a new section of tunnel had been dug out, the shield was driven forwards and the surface behind it lined with brick.

Brunel's iron tunnelling shield was three storeys high and contained 36 chambers. Each chamber could hold one worker.

Tunnel boring machines

Today, tunnels are dug using giant tunnel boring machines (TBMs). Hydraulic rams press the cutting wheel against the tunnel face. A giant rotating head at the front cuts into the rock, and a conveyor belt at the back carries the rock away. For each new project, a custom-built TBM is made, to the exact size needed for the tunnel. One of the largest TBMs ever made, nicknamed Bertha, has a diameter of 17.45 m.

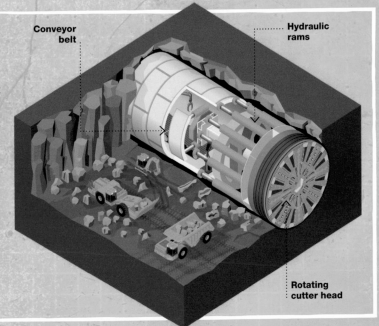

Conveyor belt

Hydraulic rams

Rotating cutter head

This is the cutting wheel of a TBM. It is fitted with cutters and scraping tools to loosen material.

PROJECT: TWISTER

Let's investigate boring methods. Place slices of a potato about 3 cm thick on a cutting board. The aim is to bore a hole through it.

You will need: a potato, straws, a pencil

Try the following methods:
1. Twist and push a straw or pencil on the potato.
2. Jam the straw or pencil to force it through the potato.
3. Plug the end of the straw with your finger and jam the straw through.

Which method works best? Why do you think this is?

SPREADING THE LOAD

When building bridges, engineers need to ensure that the weight of the bridge is supported. Parts are stretched, while others are squashed. For the bridge to stay up, it must balance both these forces.

John Roebling (1806–1869)

American, John Roebling, designed the Brooklyn Bridge in New York, USA. Both a suspension bridge and cable-stayed, it was the first bridge to be made using steel-wire suspension. Roebling died after an accident while surveying the site, and the project was finished by his son, Washington. The bridge took 14 years to complete, opening in 1883.

The Brooklyn Bridge connects Manhattan to Brooklyn across the East River.

Suspension bridge

Cables are suspended between towers. Suspenders attach the cables to the deck to support it. The cables are under tension (stretched), while the towers are compressed.

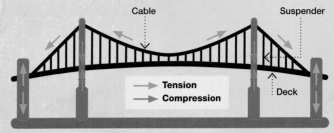

Beam bridge

The deck is a straight beam that is under tension. It is usually placed on top of piers that are under compression. Simple beam bridges with no piers are made to span short distances. The simplest form of a beam bridge is a log bridge built over a stream.

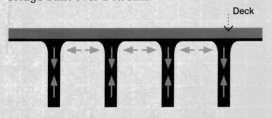

Deck

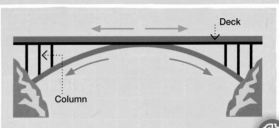

Arch bridge

The supporting arch is under compression while the deck is under tension. The arch directs force to the sides. Arch bridges need strong rock on either side to support the compression of the arch.

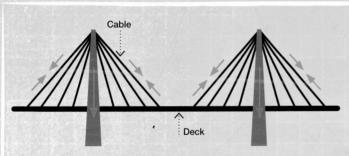

Cable

Deck

Cable-stayed bridge

The deck is supported by a series of cables suspended from towers. The cables are under tension while the towers are compressed.

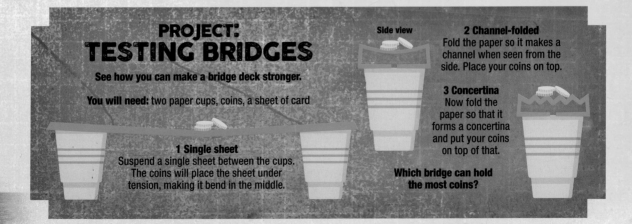

PROJECT:
TESTING BRIDGES

See how you can make a bridge deck stronger.

You will need: two paper cups, coins, a sheet of card

Side view

2 Channel-folded
Fold the paper so it makes a channel when seen from the side. Place your coins on top.

3 Concertina
Now fold the paper so that it forms a concertina and put your coins on top of that.

1 Single sheet
Suspend a single sheet between the cups. The coins will place the sheet under tension, making it bend in the middle.

Which bridge can hold the most coins?

TOWERING GIANTS

Built for the Paris Exhibition in 1889, the Eiffel Tower is a four-sided pyramid made of wrought iron. The tower gains its strength by fixing its 15,000 pieces into a frame of parallelograms and triangles. The 186 triangles spread the weight evenly, making the structure extremely strong, while using a minimum of material.

Gustav Eiffel (1832–1923)

Eiffel was a French civil engineer who built many iron viaducts and bridges around France, using his knowledge of the properties of triangles to make strong but light structures that would withstand the wind and rain.

If all the iron that constructs the Eiffel Tower were to be melted down, it would form a solid block covering the size of its square base, just 5 cm thick.

Growing taller

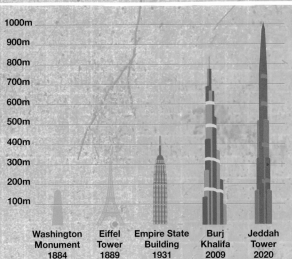

Washington Monument 1884 (169 m)	Eiffel Tower 1889 (324 m)	Empire State Building 1931 (443 m)	Burj Khalifa 2009 (838 m)	Jeddah Tower 2020 (1,000 m)

When it was completed in 1889, the 324-m-high Eiffel Tower was the tallest manmade structure in the world. Today it is dwarfed by the highest skyscrapers. The tallest building is currently the 838-m-high Burj Khalifa in Dubai, but the Jeddah Tower in Saudi Arabia is planned to stand one km high when it is completed in 2020.

PROJECT: TOWER IT UP

To see how good triangles are in spreading a load, try making your own paper tower out of triangular structures. See how high you can go.

You will need: paper, scissors, tape, biscuits

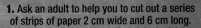

1. Ask an adult to help you to cut out a series of strips of paper 2 cm wide and 6 cm long.
2. Build a supply of triangular bricks by folding the strips into thirds and taping the open edges together.
3. Build the tower with layers of triangles. Place the triangles alternately tip side up and tip side down, as shown above. Separate each level with layers of unfolded planks.

Test the strength of your tower by balancing biscuits on it.

LINKING THE OCEANS

The Panama Canal opened in 1914. It cut across the centre of Panama, linking the Atlantic and Pacific Oceans so that ships could avoid the dangerous route around South America. The canal was built by the US, following a failed attempt by the French. It took nearly ten years to build and required tens of thousands of workers.

John Frank Stevens (1853–1943)

Stevens (left) was the American engineer in charge of planning the canal. While the French had attempted to build a sea-level dam, cutting out a flat route, Stevens decided that it was necessary to raise the canal above sea level and build a system of lakes and locks to carry ships along it.

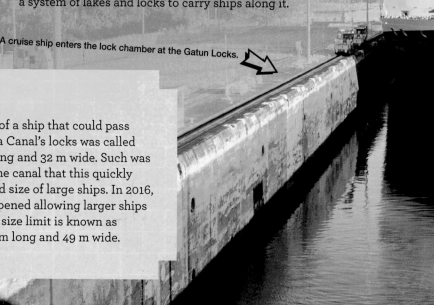

A cruise ship enters the lock chamber at the Gatun Locks.

Panamax

The maximum size of a ship that could pass through the Panama Canal's locks was called 'Panamax': 294 m long and 32 m wide. Such was the importance of the canal that this quickly became the standard size of large ships. In 2016, a new set of locks opened allowing larger ships through. The larger size limit is known as New Panamax: 366 m long and 49 m wide.

Up and over

The Panama Canal is 77 km long. Three locks at either side raise ships 26 m above sea level to an artificial lake in the middle of the canal called Gatun Lake.

The lake provides a reservoir of water for use in the locks. It was made by damming the River Chagres.

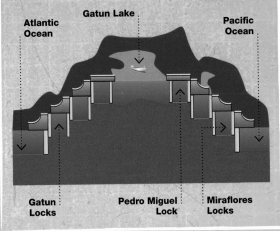

Atlantic Ocean

Gatun Lake

Pacific Ocean

Gatun Locks

Pedro Miguel Lock

Miraflores Locks

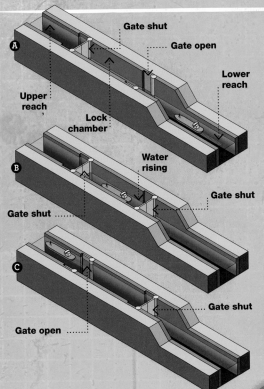

A

Upper reach

Lock chamber

Gate shut

Gate open

Lower reach

B

Gate shut

Water rising

Gate shut

C

Gate open

Gate shut

How locks work

Locks raise or lower ships in a canal. To move up a lock, a ship enters the lock chamber and the bottom gate is closed behind it (A). Water pours into the lock from above, raising the level of the water until it is equal to the level at the top gate (B). The top gate is opened and the ship moves out at the raised level (C).

PROJECT: MAKE YOUR OWN LAKE

See how you can make an artificial lake.

You will need:
a large plastic container, sand, ice lolly sticks, small stones, water

1. Fill the plastic container with sand and dig out the path of a river from one end to the other.

2. Choose a place to dam your river, and build up a dam using lolly sticks and stones.

3. Make your dam a triangular shape so that it is stronger at the bottom.

Now test out your dam by pouring water into the river. To create a lake, the dam will need to let a little water through but not too much.

BUILDING
HIGH IN THE SKY

The word 'skyscraper' was first used in the 1880s to describe buildings with more than 10 floors. Today there are more than 20 buildings in the world with more than 100 floors. The oldest of these is the Empire State Building in New York.

Steel frame

American chief architect William F. Lamb (1893–1952) chose a design in which the strength of the building was provided by a metal frame made from huge 40-tonne steel beams. The limestone walls were hung from the frame. These are known as curtain walls as they do not bear any of the load. This is now the standard way to build very tall buildings.

The workers who secured the steel beams in place amazed onlookers with their fearless approach to working high in the sky.

Completed in 1931, the 102-storey 443-m-high Empire State Building was the tallest skyscraper in the world for 40 years.

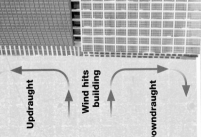

Downdraughts

Tall buildings such as the one on the left often create strong winds at street level. This is caused when air hits the building and is pushed downwards. In New York, the Flatiron Building, built in 1903, became notorious for gusts of wind that would lift up the skirts of women walking past it. Today, architects test their designs in wind tunnels to avoid producing unwanted winds.

Updraught

Wind hits building

Downdraught

Mass damper

Strong winds are not just a nuisance at street level. They can be a danger to the whole building. The 509-m-high Taipei 101 building in Taiwan counters the effects of dangerous winds using a device called a tuned mass damper. This 660-tonne steel pendulum is suspended from the 91st floor. It sways to offset any movement of the building.

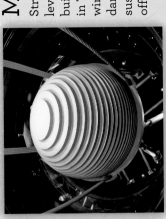

PROJECT:
LEAN ON ME

Some shapes create stronger columns than others. See how strong you can make a piece of paper.

You will need: paper, tape, a pile of books

1. Make three different shapes out of three large sheets of paper: a triangular column, a square column and a circular column.

2. Test your columns by seeing how many books you can balance on them before they collapse.

Which shape is the strongest?

HOLDING BACK THE FLOW

Dams are built on rivers to create reservoirs for water supply, to protect against flooding or to generate electricity through hydroelectric power.

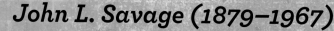

John L. Savage (1879–1967)

Savage was the chief engineer in charge of building the Hoover Dam in the USA. Working for the US government, Savage designed several other dams and canal systems in the US. In 1947, he began work in China to dam the River Yangtze, but the project was abandoned. Nearly 60 years later, the Three Gorges Dam was completed on the same site, creating the largest electricity power plant in the world.

Hoover Dam

This 221-m-high arch-gravity dam was opened in 1936. It was built across the Colorado River. The dam created the 180-km-long Lake Mead, the largest reservoir in the US, providing water to 20 million people. At the foot of the dam is a power station. Water gushes through its turbines at 140 km/h, generating enough electricity for 1.3 million people.

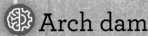

Arch dam

The concrete dam arches into the reservoir. Forces are transferred to the rock on either side of the dam. Arch dams are built in canyons with solid rock walls that can resist the pressure.

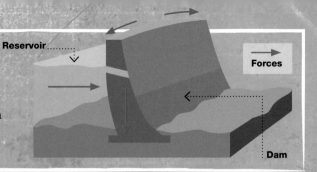

Reservoir

Forces

Dam

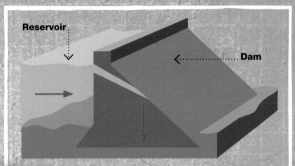

Reservoir

Dam

Gravity dam

These heavy concrete structures are designed to transfer the entire load of the water downwards. They are often built to span narrow valleys.

Buttress dam

Similar to a gravity dam, but reinforced with supports, or buttresses, that help to hold back the force of the water. The load is transferred both downwards and into the buttresses.

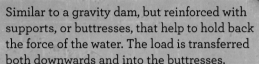

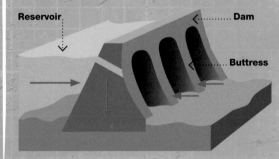

Reservoir

Dam

Buttress

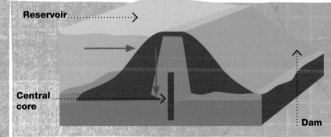

Reservoir

Central core

Dam

Embankment dam

Made of earth or rock, embankment dams transfer the weight downwards. This kind of dam is often built for flood control.

PROJECT:
UNDER PRESSURE

The turbines in a dam are placed near the bottom, find out why with this investigation.

You will need: a 2-litre plastic drinks bottle, a small drill bit, water, tape, bucket

1. Ask an adult to make four small holes, evenly spaced in a line up one side of the bottle with the drill bit.

2. Cover the holes with tape and fill the bottle with water.

3. Hold the bottle over a bucket or sink and take the tape off the holes. Water will stream out of the holes.

Which hole has the fastest stream of water?

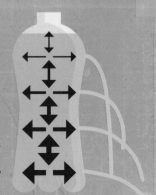

POWER FROM THE WIND

People have harnessed the power of the wind for centuries using windmills. Modern wind turbines are much more powerful, and are used to generate electricity in a clean, renewable way. The first wind turbine capable of generating more than 1 megawatt (1 million watts) of power was designed in 1941 by American engineer Palmer Cosslett Putnam.

Turbine evolution

Putnam's wind turbine (left) had two 20-m-long blades. It broke down after about 1,000 hours of operation and was never fully repaired. It was dismantled in 1946. A wind turbine of this size was not built again until 1979. Today's turbines have three blades, which are shaped to give maximum power. The curved blades are designed with a shape called an aerofoil. An aerofoil creates a force called lift, which pushes the blades up.

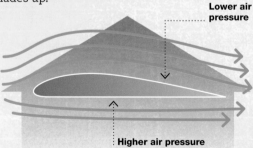

Lower air pressure

Higher air pressure

Air moving over an aerofoil moves faster than the air moving under it. This creates lower pressure above the blade than below it, generating lift.

Wind farms

In areas with regularly high winds, wind turbines are grouped together into wind farms. The turbines in wind farms must be placed at least five blade-lengths apart so that they do not interfere with one another.

The London Array is the largest off-shore wind farm in the world. Located in the Thames Estuary near London, it contains 175 turbines.

PROJECT:
SPIN ME ROUND

Make a pinwheel turbine out of a piece of paper to see how wind blowing in different directions will spin the pinwheel in different ways.

You will need:
a piece of paper, a ruler, a pencil, scissors, a skewer, a hair dryer

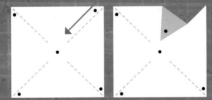

1. Cut the paper into a square with 20 cm sides.
2. Fold the square along a diagonal, then fold it along the other diagonal.
3. About 5 cm from the centre, make a small mark on each crease. Cut along the folds to the mark.
4. With the skewer, make four holes to the right of each crease near the corners and a hole in the centre.
5. Push the skewer through the centre hole and fold each piece over so that the holes at the corners are all on top of one another.

Use the hair dryer on a low setting to test your pinwheel. Make a prediction which way it will turn. Were you right? Which angle makes the pinwheel spin fastest? Is it more effective when you blow into the cupped parts of the pinwheel's blades? Can you make it turn in the other direction?

ZERO-GRAVITY ENGINEERING

Some scientists spend months at a time living and working in space stations such as the International Space Station. Space engineers face many problems when designing modules for people to live in the 'zero-gravity' conditions. Simple things such as eating, sleeping and using the toilet can be very difficult when there is nothing to hold stuff down.

Tortillas are good food for space as they don't create crumbs that will float away. In zero-gravity, tables can be placed at any angle so that you can reach things more easily.

Space design

Architect Galina Balashova worked for the Soviet space programme, designing the living spaces for the Soyuz spacecraft of the 1960s and 1970s. Her designs helped cosmonauts (Russian for 'astronauts') overcome the confusing effects of zero-gravity. The ceilings were brightly coloured and the floor dark to create a sense of up and down. Balashova also designed deep zero-gravity bucket seats that are still used today.

Balashova made really detailed colour drawings of her designs.

Science in space

Scientists can find out many interesting things from experiments in zero-gravity conditions. Candles have been found to burn very differently in space. With Earth's gravity, the hot gas rises, pulling in cool air underneath it, as shown below left. This provides a source of oxygen to keep the candle wax burning. With no gravity, the hot gas does not rise, so the candle burns slowly with a small, round flame (below right). Engineers study how different fuels burn in space, and use this knowledge to design more efficient engines for cars or aircraft.

PROJECT:
THE GRAVITY EFFECT

Astronauts in orbit still feel the effects of Earth's gravity, but their orbit is a form of free fall. Everything is falling at the same time, and this creates a feeling of weightlessness. You can see how this works very easily.

You will need:
a paper cup, water, a bucket or sink

1. Poke a small hole in the side of the cup near the bottom.
2. Fill the cup with water, holding your finger over the hole. Let go of the hole over the bucket and see how the water pours out.
3. Now fill the cup the same way, holding your finger over the hole, but this time let go of the cup as you take your finger off and let it drop into the bucket.

What happens now?

GET READY FOR TAKE-OFF

When building airport runways, engineers must take many factors into account. They need to build the runway to minimise the chance of dangerous cross-winds. The runways must provide good grip for the aircraft wheels, and need to be as flat as possible.

⚙️ Runways

Runways are given a number between 01 and 36 indicating the direction they are pointing. A runway 01 points at magnetic north, 09 points east, 18 south and 27 west. This allows pilots to line up their planes correctly as they come in to land. It is safest for planes to take off and land into the wind, and larger airports have several runways pointing in different directions.

When planes land on a ship, the ship will always turn to face the wind. Pilots land by flying directly into the wind, knowing that the runway will be lined up.

Flying high

Altitude is a crucial factor when building a runway. It is harder to take off in thinner air, so the higher the airport, the longer its runways need to be. The longest runway in the world is at Qamdo Bamda Airport in Tibet, at an altitude of 4,400 m. Its runway is 5,500 m long – 50 per cent longer than is needed at sea level.

Runway on stilts

Squeezed between the ocean and a mountain range, Funchal Airport in Madeira was one of the most perilous airports in the world, with a short runway and hazards on either side. The runway was extended in 1986 by building a platform supported by 180 70-m-tall columns. A main road runs underneath the runway. This novel solution was engineered by Brazilian firm Andrade Gutierrez.

PROJECT:
PAPER PLANES

Planes landing into the wind maximise the force called drag, which slows them down. When making paper planes, you do not want too much drag as they will not fly very far. But you need enough lift to keep the plane in the air. The power of your throw gives the plane a force called thrust. Some of that thrust produces lift. Make paper planes of different shapes to see which will fly furthest, and which will stay in the air the longest.

You will need: paper

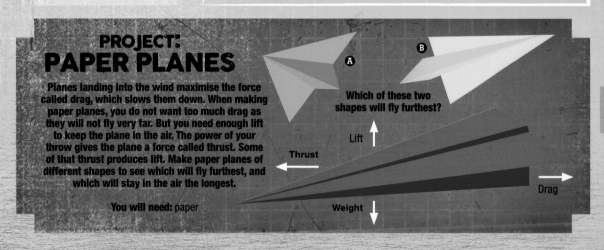

Which of these two shapes will fly furthest?

Lift

Thrust

Drag

Weight

ALTITUDE
The distance a point is above sea level.

CONCENTRIC RINGS
Circles of different sizes that have the same point as their centre.

COSMONAUT
An astronaut from the Soviet Union or Russia.

DRAG
A force that acts in the opposite direction to an object's motion, slowing it down.

HYDRAULICS
A system for operating a machine that uses liquid to transfer force from one place to another.

HYDROELECTRIC POWER
Electricity produced by moving water. The water powers turbines, whose spinning motion is turned into electricity by a generator.

LIFT
A force that acts on an object in an upwards direction.

LOCK
Part of a canal that is closed off with gates in order to raise or lower a ship, or boat, as it passes from one level to another.

MAGNETIC NORTH
The direction in which a compass needle points in response to Earth's magnetic field.

PARALLELOGRAM
A four-sided shape made from two sets of parallel lines.

PENDULUM
A weight that is hung from a fixed point so that it can swing freely.

RESERVOIR
A lake, often manmade, that is used to store water for use in homes, agriculture or industry.

THRUST
A force that acts in the same direction as an object's motion.

TURBINE
A machine that turns pressure from moving water or air into spinning motion.

ANSWERS

p.7 Ramp it up

When you lower the slope, you should need fewer coins in the cup to move the apple.

p.9 Heated needle

As the knitting needle heats up, it expands lengthways. This rolls the sewing needle, causing the straw to rotate.

p.11 How bright is the light?

The same amount of light is spread out over larger areas as you move away from the torch. The area increases in size by a square of the distance. This means that the area of light at 10 cm distance will be four times larger than the area of light at 5 cm (10^2 = 100, while 5^2 = 25).

[Maths note: The area of a circle (A) is given by the formula $A = \frac{1}{4} \pi d^2$ or $A = 0.785 \times d^2$, where d is the diameter]

p.13 Twister

Plugging the end of the straw and jamming it through works best. Air is trapped inside the straw, keeping it stiff. However, air is a gas that can be compressed, so it allows potato flesh to enter the straw.

p.15 Testing bridges

The more evenly the weight is spread across the deck, the more weight it will support. The channel-folded deck supports far more coins than the single sheet. The concertina deck supports the most coins.

p.21 Lean on me

The circular column should hold many more books than the other two shapes. It distributes the weight of the books evenly. The square and triangle concentrate the weight at their corners, which then buckle.

p.23 Under pressure

The lower the hole, the faster and stronger the stream. There is more water above the level of the hole, creating greater pressure. So turbines are placed near the bottom where the water pressure is greatest.

p.25 Spin me round

When you blow straight at the pinwheel, it spins anti-clockwise. If you turn the pinwheel to the side and blow into the cups, it will spin more quickly. If you blow into the backs of the cups, it will spin slowly clockwise.

p.27 The gravity effect

The cup and water both fall at the same rate, so no water pours out of the hole.

p.29 Paper planes

The dart-shaped plane (B) will fly faster. The glider-shaped plane (A) will stay in the air longest.

INDEX